The Theater of Night

The Theater of Night

by Alberto Ríos

COPPER CANYON PRESS

Copper Canyon Press is in residence at Fort Worden State Park in Port Townsend, Washington, under the auspices of Centrum Foundation. Centrum is a gathering place for artists and creative thinkers from around the world, students of all ages and backgrounds, and audiences seeking extraordinary cultural enrichment.

LIBRARY OF CONGRESS CATALOGING-IN-PUBLICATION DATA
Ríos, Alberto.
  The theater of night / by Alberto Ríos.
    p. cm.
  ISBN 1-55659-230-2 (hardcover : alk. paper)
  1. Mexican-American Border Region—Poetry. 2. Mexican Americans—Poetry. 3. Older people—Poetry. 4. Love poetry, American. I. Title.

PS3568.I587T47 2005
813'.54—DC22

                          2005008868

98765432 FIRST PRINTING

COPPER CANYON PRESS
Post Office Box 271
Port Townsend, Washington 98368
www.coppercanyonpress.org

For Joaquin, at 20.

This book is in good and personal debt to
Clemente and Ventura and all the rest of my
extended family, in whom so many of my words
find treasure, and to my hometown of Nogales.

Acknowledgments

Earlier versions of the poems appeared in the following journals, newspapers, and artist's books:

ArtLife, Atlanta Review, Bastard Review, Glimmer Train, Indiana Review, Inside Chance, Journal of Ethnic Studies, Mānoa, New York Times, Prairie Schooner, Quarterly West, Red Rock Review, Research, Ruah, Slant, Solo, Southwestern American Literature, Visiones, and *Washington Square.*

I want to thank the editors of these publications, the early readers of this collection, and Arizona State University.

Contents

SIX

ONE

Northern Desert Towns in the Turn of the Old Century

1

In town, in Cucurpe and Rayón,
In those small places and on those dirt streets

My grandmother walked with her sisters.
They were girls then, and could remember themselves laughing.

In those days there was a rabies for great civilization,
For suits, for Paris, for starch, for good grades, for musical societies.

People went to Saturday dances. Women wore their hair up.
Men walked with canes, fancy for walking but as much to hit the dogs

Biting at their capes—which the dogs thought
With all that black flailing in the summer wind

Was something attacking their masters,
The dogs having no understanding of civilized refinement,

Content themselves to walk on all fours
Unclothed, barking at will, and urinating in the neighbors' yards.

2

The invisible wall between the town and the desert,
It was the dare of the town drawn as a line in the sand,

A dare against Nature and the sun, a dare against everything
The townspeople knew and imagined in the distance,

A dare as strong in its intent as the great barricades of history,
All those stories, all those walls and wire and water,

All those protections trying to raise themselves
Against the enemy, against the distant *out-there.*

But in a later century people would come to this place anyway
In shorts, sandals, and half-sleeved shirts.

The townspeople and the visitors would watch and nod,
Looking at each other. After all this time

The desert people marveled at the *out-there*
When it came in as it should from the sun.

3

The towns in the northern desert
Had taken care of themselves.

In the middle of the desert they bloomed
And a song came up

From them, sometimes, in the evening.
Smoke rose at dinnertime, and early light.

Rain and harvesting the corn
All meant something to the town.

When the electricity came, and the new lights,
The cars and the tourists,

Everything was different. Rayón and Cucurpe,
Magdalena and Imuris, all the other small towns,

They became old, like my grandmother and her sisters.
Together they waited to see what would come next.

The Mermaid Comb

He carved the hair comb out of a cow's horn,
A mermaid comb imagined from stories

Given to all of us on star-filled summer nights
In the high desert. The *sirenas,* they were called—

The *sirenas* lived inside the water somewhere far away.
They were the opposite of us,

The way we lived without water on those mesquite hills,
These hills that were our waves, very slow

In the distance, slow but big in our ocean of air.
From beyond the horizon to the south,

From the old place that did not have a name,
Someone first brought a comb a little like this one

To be the great-grandmother of all those combs,
Those combs and their stories—

The stories were always about the girls who left
Then got lost, stories with always something of a sad look in the telling.

Nobody could say for certain about the existence of these mermaids,
So they lived very well here where we made a home for them

In our words and prayers, and on our bureaus.
But there was more.

There was the secret of the combs.
This was not a story told to us, nor one we told,

But we all knew it.
It told itself not with words but with small teeth.

I felt its bite sharply with my skin, with the small bumps
The comb raised, not just on my head but my body as well:

When I put water on my hair,
The mermaid came alive,

The comb of her tail moving like sure fingers
Through the moist dark of my loose strands,

Moving up and down, looking finally
For the topmost place to rest,

The place to stay and to see and be seen.
How else for a mermaid to behave?

And there is the matter of modesty,
Which in mermaids is not discussed

But everyone thinks the same thing—
They look and they breathe a little harder at what they see.

To wear this comb
Was to breathe a little harder, too.

When I went out like this, this comb in my hair,
I thought the *sirena* and her small chest looked like me.

I thought the carving looked a little
Like looking at myself in a mirror after a bath,

Those two curious paint spatters on my chest, those two
Flat, simple thumbs

Like the dark noses of two small dogs sniffing up
At dinner on the kitchen table.

Nights walking with this girl, this woman who looked like me,
In my hair

The desert—warm enough already—grew even warmer.
The feeling was a weight, not only on my head but on my chest,

Unbearable. I could not breathe.
I felt like I myself was underneath the faraway water.

When he carved the cow horn into a mermaid comb,
I know he was thinking of me.

When I wore the mermaid
I felt in those moments with passion

The touch of his hands,
Though he had not touched me.

Clemente, in Love, Speaks to Himself in the Mirror

We have, we are told—we are sure—five senses.
This is easy, this is first grade, this is certain.

We know this, *five*. But look, when I count
I can't stop: I see ten fingers in front of me

Plain as anything. Ten. You see them, too.
And they move around.

Someone, whoever he is,
He has been keeping something from us.

I see this, now, using my sense of cunning.
That makes six senses quickly and right there.

Clemente, they used to say, *pay attention,*
Do your work, don't look up—I know now

What they were up to. I see what they were trying
To do. But it's over. They can't stop me anymore.

I can see ten, but I can think a thousand.
The world of a thousand senses—

This opens things up considerably, don't you think?
They add up right away, and easy, these gifts of mine:

The sense of wonder, horse sense,
The sense of timing, good sense,

Sense enough to come in from the rain.
I will not be stopped. I know what I know.

I feel powerful, I am powerful—Look at me!—
I am the Sense-Man! And I am walking right past you

Straight into and ready for the world. All of you!
All of you! Out of my way!

The Pomegranate and the Big Crowd

Ventura because she was hungry and because
She was curious—but more because she was curious—

Took the dare, a kiss for a pomegranate.
Everyone gathered, her friends and his. Everyone

Watched: the boys, the girls, the pigs and the chickens,
And more. Moving to the front were the children

She and Clemente would one day have,
And the children of those children, too,

Gathered and loud with everyone and everything else,
Loud as the pigs and fast as the chickens

Though she could not see them.
Still, they crowded her, and she could feel

Their anxious breathing.
This boy Clemente whom she would kiss

She would have kissed even without the pomegranate,
Though she could not say it

And was glad of this game. He suited her,
She thought. He had a strong face.

He felt what she felt. She could see him look around
But not at their friends. She could see him

Feel the shiver of the children they would have:
Their son Margarito, his two sisters

Both of whom would become nuns
If just to pray enough to take care of him,

This boy so serious he would seem like a stranger
In their arms, serious enough by himself

To make up for Clemente and Ventura
And for all the laughter

They themselves would feel,
This curious child who, as an old man

Would never trust a doctor for anything.
And his serious wife to come, Refugio,

And her sisters, Matilde and Consuelo as well,
All the people who would follow this kiss,

So many of them, and their children, too,
Everyone stood there, arms up, everyone watching,

So much noise in this moment,
This quick lending of herself

To his cheek, the way Ventura would later kiss
All these impatient children of theirs. The kiss

Seemed so small, but was filled with itself.
This small moment of affection she gave this boy

The quarter-second that it took:
There they all stood, waiting with the crowd

Egging them on, hefting the pomegranate
And pushing them toward each other.

Clemente and Ventura in that quarter-second lived
Their lives, a quarter-second not finished yet.

I Heard Him with My Back

He spoke to me through my back.
I heard him as loudly as if he had put his mouth to my ear.

The trick at first was easy enough,
His writing letters and then words on the full of my skin

As I lay with him but faced away,
Pretending a small fight or some petulance or sleepiness.

Then it was when we were standing,
Alone at first and I was laughing quietly at what he was saying

In this easy language.
But after that he began to make me laugh, too,

Outside, when we would stand with small groups
Making ourselves invisible in the crowds of the plaza.

But then it was in our living rooms,
Standing with our parents and everyone else,

Standing with the neighbors, all dressed up—
And him, saying what he was saying,

Loud as anything there on my back.
After all our days and months together,

My back heard him better than my ears.
My back understood his hands.

When he spoke to me like he did and where he did
As we stood in these living rooms in front of everyone,

He made my mouth make a noise.
My half-words made no sense to anyone, so they would hush me.

They would give me looks with their eyebrows tight and low.
These noises made no sense,

These small, volcanic risings that came out of me,
They made no sense to anyone but him.

He knew what I was saying, what I meant,
What I could not help but say.

I was answering his questions
Right there in front of the world and in the open air.

Right there I answered him.
This was at first, before we married.

After the months and then years of learning this alphabet,
I could hear his hand even when it was not on my back.

I could sense it coming to my back when he was behind me.
I began to feel it

Even when he was across the room from me.
He would look at me but his look was not hard, not like the others'.

When I would see him looking at me that way—
I felt that look too as his hand on my back.

It began to happen later even as I heard his voice from another room,
That his voice came through the doorway to me,

That his voice came through the walls to me,
That it reached my back as his hand.

Finally, through the years,
That voice did not stop at my back—it entered me

Through the shoulder blades
And made its way into my spine and then into my dreams.

It was his hand, and it spoke
All these years what his mouth could not say.

Mesquite Coyotes

1

In the Sonora, in the desert
Beyond the outskirts of the northern desert towns,

In the scruff and scrub, the creosote and dark sand,
Everything is something else:

Leaves are something else—they are needles and pins
On the trees. The trees themselves are something else,

Something, something thin, something animal and hungry.
Each tree—the trees that are beasts as well in the desert—

Each tree keeps its distance far away from any other:
On the edges of these towns there is an invisible wall.

The law of nature is simple, is the first line
In the constitution that governs this place:

Walk beyond the wall and you walk
On the ground of the other world.

2

In the desert, trees out there are not trees—
They are animals no less than wolves,

Animals no less than coyotes,
With teeth just as sharp, with appetites just as large.

But the trees are smarter than the beasts.
The animals out there die fast.

They eat and get eaten.
The trees, the trees, however, they pretend not to move.

They disguise themselves as trees.
Taking a step takes years,

So they are careful. And because they give shade,
However meager, everyone sits under them,

So the trees have overheard all the plans
Through all the years. They know what to do.

3

The animals in turn are not animals here.
They do not have and never have had the luxury to stop

And give themselves names,
To stop for the photographers and biographers

Who are always asking questions
But who might also be hunters—

People, the animals know, spend much of their time
Trying to fool them into putting a foot

Into something that hurts. People, they know, want them
To stop long enough

For the sudden gunshot or arrow, that fast
Feeling that makes them fall.

Animals, animals and trees,
Animals and trees and people, finally,

They learned to hide here, and not simply from the sun,
Which should have been the worst thing.

Clemente's Red Horse

1

People think I'm crazy—
Nobody else saw the red horse.

They saw only the same horse,
The same beast they had always seen

No matter how hard
I tried to explain.

This carving of a red horse
I hold in my hand,

I made it from memory,
I made it from having seen

A red horse one morning
Remarkable in the distance.

Red—the horse was this color of red,
Bright and near to fire,

Not the simple brown color
That can sometimes turn on itself,

That pretend-red.
The horse was red

Not before or after this moment,
But it was red at that moment I saw it.

The sun rising shone
A particular light on the horse.

It made a different horse in its place
As it stood and looked at me.

That light made the animal red,
Red on the inside and outside both.

Red was the only way I could see it
From then on.

The horse itself, which was brown,
Was lost to me soon thereafter.

2

But the red *horse-of-the-moment*
Lives still.

Where there had been one horse,
Suddenly for me there were two,

But in the same space.
The horse was unexpectedly bigger to me

Though it had not grown.
I hold some of that horse now in my hands.

People think I'm crazy—
Nobody else saw the red horse,

They say, and they don't want to hear about it.
They think it has nothing to do with them.

They don't have time.
They're busy with something of their own, busy

Thinking about the yellow tree
They have inside themselves,

Even after all these years,
The tree that turned butter yellow,

Once, in their childhood,
Yellow altogether one moody dusk,

A sudden color they never forgot.
A yellow tree

Or a shimmering, old-orange hillside—
They each have something.

I have not seen their secrets,
The same way they have not seen the horse,

But I know they have them.
I carved the red horse

To show them what I know.
They only pretend not to recognize it.

3

They shake their heads
As if they don't know what I am talking about.

But a red horse, it stops you.
It makes you laugh, at the very least.

It stops you from moving along the street
The way you had intended.

It makes you think, *that's impossible,*
But you are face-to-face with it.

These moments aren't only the sun's doing—
Other things conspire as well.

The moon, too, more than once has given me
A luminous gray house,

A house not my own but in the same spot,
Making where I live seem twice as big,

Just like the horse,
My one house suddenly two different houses.

And the wind, too, lends itself to this work.
The wind has bent the world,

And taken away the weak parts—
It makes me close my eyes when it blows

But I have seen it. The stars, too,
The way they move around in the sky—

They're up to something.
I don't know what. I don't know

More than to paint a horse red, finally,
And understand that I live in many places here.

People think I'm crazy.
Still, they don't go on for too long.

We argue about the red horse.
But the red horse, there it is.

A Chance Witnessing of the Morning Animal

The mid-January day's morning
Light comes slowly, stretching itself

Before standing, arms first, hands next,
Fingers beyond that, nails even farther.

In this light, this bare stretch of light out of dark,
The sun catches with its sharp reaches

The top of the heights of the trees first,
The highest single leaves caught in slivers and crisp,

Sudden and barely as if they were a mouse
Each one, illuminated in the talons of a rising hawk,

Some white suddenly, and some red and some brown,
With a slight flutter of movement in the high breeze,

Each of the tops of these apricot and peach and pecan,
The tops of the desert plum in this far cold end of autumn,

Everything helpless in those first wild
Leafless few seconds of morning,

The light shining just across
The highest tips of the leaves, then into them,

Through them, into their suddenly disembodied twigs,
The bones of the leaves pierced with radiance, severed,

Floating in the barbed animal grasp of this momentary light,
Lifted up, almost, lifted up and apart from this world

Until not a second later the great tide of light
Finds in everything the beginnings of its vast shore—

And the first wave makes its crash,
A crash so great that sound cannot serve it.

TWO

They Said I Was a Crying Bride

Mr. and Mrs. Clemente Ríos—
Had anything ever sounded so evening and elegant,

Words from lifetimes of behaving. These were quiet
Words—*Mr.* and *Mrs.*—but sitting on the lap of Uncle Thrill,

Whispered to me in church by Cousin Hand:
As I helped to cook in the kitchen on a Sunday,

My hands were full of salt, but in me
I was full not of bones but of feeling,

A scaffolding of my shape
Made with all the little pins they put in new shirts.

It was one thing to look at the outside of my hand
But something else to look on the inside.

Mr. and Mrs. Clemente Ríos—
It was a marriage into this family

On the outside—salt, something regular,
Just a wedding, like air and like water, something

Regular and quiet in this way
To the world which made its rules.

But in me was a deeper shore
On whose edge I stood

Looking out toward the farther inside.
I could see Clemente sometimes

In a soaring boat. When he came to me
He was wet, some of that ocean

Falling from so much of itself through my eyes.
It was not unhappiness.

Had I a mountain terrain
Inside myself, rather than an ocean,

Were he a sawyer and not a mariner,
Then the water would be something else,

Something that had clung to him from the trees.
Pine needles instead would fall from my eyes,

Pine and sap, scent and June beetles.
It was only luck that this was not the case,

That instead of flying, instead of shouting,
Instead of all the things that could have

Come from my eyes, the water being water
Was so easily explained as tears.

The River Was Their Honeymoon

Small and slight, quiet and under-stars as it seemed,
A whisper to anyone else, a nothing, a task, a place for ghosts,

The river was everything for the two of them,
Their honeymoon every time, new every time

The way the water in the river was new every time.
Their river started as this small creek

But the closer they walked toward it the more it seemed to change—
It was a mighty river, then, a great wave

And ripple, and ripple again, that ran through Paris, and Madrid,
London and Africa and to the south, a river with many names,

Many disguises, many passports and languages, the Seine,
The Nile, the Thames, the Volga, the Amazon,

A river that wound around through narrow cities and tapered shores,
Passing through them and beyond, spilling

Into the great wide plains of so many places, this water
A mercy of the desert, this water the blood of the moment, this water

The untempered vocabulary they spoke, or that spoke them,
This river, it slowed after all—though it had seemed altogether unable,

So much was its movement and its blunt forwardness, its riverness—
But it slowed after all and made everything, including them,

Riverine, slow and wide, and became evening and became night,
Slowed into itself, into memory, into finally what was the drink of water

They shared from their hands, the drink of water and goodnight,
The river that was everyone's and not just theirs, regular,

The river that everyone saw and walked past, a little hurriedly,
A little scared after all to see anything that might call out to them.

A Marrow of Water

Somewhere along she had begun to feel
She had clouds for bones—

They were white, and in bone shapes,
But they would not stay.

They moved, out, beyond her.
They moved over and let him in a little.

When she first saw him, when he stood
Next to her, he stood slightly inside her

As if the lines of their bodies
Blurred briefly, his arm inside hers,

His hip as she passed him
A little in the middle of her walk.

He put himself in her
And she did not let him out.

He moved around in her, she felt it,
Inside her but everywhere.

It was just in her dreams at first,
Then in her bones.

And inside her eyes, inside and outside
Both, it was him standing there:

She could close her eyes
And see him caught inside them.

She didn't understand this, she didn't know
This would happen.

The Light Brown Map

The west of her was arm
And the east as well,

As she lay fallen on her back in the bed.
The north was forest, was jungle,

All tangle and light moisture.
The south was—what might one guess?

What might feet resemble
In this great game of the darkened room?

If there was her in all directions,
I say, if she was the map itself

In that moment of crucial positioning,
If hair was north and arms were sideways,

Then feet were South America, or Africa,
Depending on the hemisphere,

The map to me was clear. If I was lost
When I started, asking permission,

Asking directions, if I was a sailor
Lost on the great ocean of this one moment,

This moment built of centuries, I later found
My way, using as a curious but sure compass

The north star of her fast breathing,
Her breathing and my closed eyes to see.

My Husband Clemente

I saw Clemente this morning in a dream.
It was him, Clemente, but when he was young.

I knew the hard, animal bones of his face.
I went to school with a boy like that and I have an uncle, too.

You've seen them, people with so much horse in them still
Even after centuries, so much horse and donkey

In the strong ones, so much spider
In the skinny ones, the way their thin fingers

Move over a piece of chicken.
And it's not just animal bones in them, animals

And spiders, smooth fish and round tortoises.
These people, they have horse dreams inside, too,

Dream pouches like organs themselves, tucked in
Along with the kidneys and the liver, a third lung,

Pouches and notes, reminders pushed in and held
In between some nerves, those nerves crisscrossed

Like rubber bands around a package.
I saw inside Clemente something of all this,

But when I awoke and looked at him again
He was still some of the Clemente from the dream.

Some of it had come back with him,
On purpose or by accident, there it was

The way the first fish flipped itself or was flipped
Onto land, the way it moved, and then walked,

Like that this bit of dream had come, into light.
With its own arms it had held on to Clemente's wide back

And hid itself in the big inside of that man.
It moved and it walked and it looked out

From his human eye and his horse eye. I was not scared.
We said no words, how foolish that would have been.

I took Clemente's big hand, to my mouth and to my hip.
It was this that he understood, and I knew it.

The Song of His Hands

I didn't care so much
About the things he said to me.

I just liked to watch
His mouth move, I liked

The music that came out of him.
If he thought I believed what he was saying

He was crazy. I never listened to him.
I only watched. His words—

Those big words came to me as big hands,
His hands themselves came to me as music,

And their songs on my face made me laugh.
He mixed up the world for me,

But when it was him I was all right.
We were both all right then.

Aunt Matilde's Story of the Big Day

The day was big, the way some days are,
The way they don't fit into themselves,

The way sometimes I think I'm too fat
And don't fit into my dresses, not right—

I think you know what I'm talking about.
I'm talking about days so large and with so many hours

You talk about days like these on other days
That don't themselves quite fill up, not enough,

Days you know that are like rolls
That could use more butter on them,

Days that aren't quite enough themselves.
On small days like that you talk about big days

And it all evens out after about a year,
Which is lucky because years are different:

They have to fit into themselves,
Though even that isn't so true anymore,

Not the more I live because I think it's true now
Some years are like some days, they're just big,

And some years really don't matter too much,
So maybe it all evens out after a century

Because centuries have to fit into themselves,
Though as I get closer to the end of this one

I don't see that it's really going to end.
I started to say this was a big day

I was going to talk about, you know the kind.
Come back and you'll see.

It's got horses in it, and your uncle's ranch.
And Santa Teresa, who went there and made a miracle happen.

Santa Teresa in Nogales

In the late 1800s in northern Mexico, Teresa Urrea, called the Saint of Cabora, fell into a cataleptic state that lasted three months and eighteen days, after which she began performing healings, which many called miracles, by laying her hands on sickness and sorrow.

1

Santa Teresita cured me of myself.
I was young, and she did what nobody else could.

She took something off of me, something from me,
And out of me, something nobody else could see.

I was an impossible case.
To do this would have seemed ill-conceived.

She gave me nothing more than the touch of her lips
Against my ear:

Those words so much, they so filled me,
They took the place of what was there.

In my troubles
I was someone else to myself, a stranger,

Another woman, someone else altogether.
In the mirror I was like a tree

In the distance,
A tree you see and have seen,

A tree you recognize
But whose name is unknown to you.

2

Teresita gathered the protections we needed,
The *milagro* figure of a whole person,

That crude tin form of the other person
I saw in myself.

Together Teresita and I made crosses with salt
In the doorways.

My mother had already put plants in the front garden,
Albahaca, romero, and *ruda.* Those three:

Sweet basil, rosemary, and rue.
Teresita did not believe in them, but she said nothing.

Nobody believed in them, but nobody was sure.
Their use came to us from the centuries before,

And their story was told at night.
When the moment came,

Santa Teresita took that thing I was, looked straight at it—
She did not flinch—

Then she showed me what to do with it,
And I did.

3

Who I had been lay at my feet. I could see me
Fall from myself

Like a dress slipped off for the night,
The two straps, once undone,

Letting everything fall to the floor in a rush.
I was left standing and fallen both,

But since I could see myself on the floor
I could tell I had stayed with the woman left standing.

This was a miracle for me.
This was a miracle for Teresita, and a pity

Nobody else was there to see.
We called her Santa Teresa anyway,

Everybody did, and the name followed her.
She left with her father soon thereafter.

I read about her in the newspapers, then lost track.
My new life, finally, spoke for itself.

It took care of remembering her even if I could not.
Everybody knew my change and her visit were the same.

4

I thought I had left that woman who was also me
On the ground that night,

But I have seen her through the years
Walking in front of me on the street.

I recognize the back of her head. I know
The way she walks by the way it feels to me when I see it.

I am filled with wanting to know how she is,
What has happened to her after all this time.

Then I remember what Teresita said to me.
It was not much, but what she said was enough—

The words themselves I have in fact forgotten,
But the feeling in them,

As if they were not words at all
But the things those words were,

That secret, that reassurance, that pair of hands
That were Teresita's lips reached inside to hold me,

That's what I remember,
So that when I see myself in the distance

I try not to call out, for fear
I will turn around.

THREE

What He Does to Me

He's a hard one. I can't explain him.
But there's something.
He's not sweet like the skin of a candy,
But he knows something about its heart.
It's on the inside with him, not on the outside.
He doesn't say *thank you* with words—
It's in his eyebrows.
Oh, I'm letting him off easy, I know.
But with him it is easy.
In all our years together,
I thought this was strange for a long time,
He has never said *bless you* when I've sneezed.
But when I've sneezed, he's never failed
To put his hand, just for a moment, on my back.
Maybe not at that moment, but here's the thing.
If he is sitting down and I'm in the kitchen,
He's never forgotten sometime later in the day
To put his hand there, right in the middle of my back,
Even hours later.
It comes to me as a surprise, sometimes,
When he does it—just the way a sneeze comes out.
Instead of a loud thing, however,
It's soft, this touching of my back.
It's soft but I feel it loud inside.

Who Had Been Friendly Now Strangers and Hard Work

When she had one baby
She had three, her two breasts

Also new, children themselves
Untamed and with lives of their own—

The sure way they filled, the way
As a child herself

She had put flour into burlap sacks,
That's how they felt, how they behaved,

The scientific way they moved,
Toward the earth

As if they were two swollen, sure
Arms of an ancient compass,

Pointing her all the time to sit, to lie down,
Though she could not stop her work.

The way she moved with them,
Danced them,

Kept them close to her,
They were like two more elbows,

The kind made when the arm is bent,
Insistent elbows

Dark-skinned at the bend.
They tried to speak in other ways, too,

Along with her child, she said,
But one had to pay attention.

Theirs was a noise for the eyes
As much as the ears.

Their words were spoken
Through a purple calligraphy,

An arrangement of lines,
Chinese characters finely drawn,

Cartographers' topographic measures,
Circle upon imperfect circle,

Stamp cancellations from far away,
Laundry marks from thin pens,

The way caliche dirt looks after a drought,
Straight lines broken into a thousand pieces,

Full Roman letters and Arabic numerals,
Roots, but growing up, not down,

As if there were a plant, a tree
Somewhere inside her:

Her veins through the months
Stretched out like a fist into fingers,

Rising to a readable surface,
A message to those who would look,

Something made of full words and near
Complete sentences

Under the paper of her skin.
The words at first looked odd to her,

Backward and not from the dictionary.
The words, however, were not less clear.

Instead, something in them moved to her,
Though she could not translate

What at first she had complained about.
She hummed all the time now,

As if she were filled with a small motor.
She offered to the world in this way

What her body spoke,
And who needed to hear, heard.

The Blurred Woman in the Photograph

She walks on five legs, this woman,
And lifts her baby with twelve arms.
She has one eye—it is her entire body:
With it she sees through strangers
And around corners.
Her skin covers the baby still:
She knows quicker than the child
The child is cold.
This woman's kiss, when it makes its slight noise
On the baby's cheek, sings
With the voices she has heard
In the lifetimes that are hers,
The music she has imagined,
The song she is hearing,
The lives in her life in a chorus.
The sound of her kiss is a white noise
Full of centuries, spare in its sound
Only from the weight of so much
This, forging its diamond in a moment.

Noise from the Sea

Her skin was the shore
Of her
And inside was ocean.
There were islands,
Places inside her
To live:
He had stood there
Inside her.
With his head to her stomach
He could make out
The ocean's noise,
In her breasts
He could make
Small waves.
When she cried
It was not her,
It was the storms of the sea
And the water
At her eye
Was the very tip
Of the highest wave
Coming out
Farther than she could hold.

The Kitchen Talk of *Comadres* Regarding a Certain Problem

Listen to me.
A woman's got to build a house

So that she's got something to walk out of
When she's ready to leave.

You say it so well, *comadre.*
You make me laugh. But I understand.

I didn't know this would happen. But the thing is,
The house I built I built with him.

This small difficulty now, however,
This beast that has come to visit us,

This beast I am telling you about—
It has become a guest I do not want.

This animal is difficult to describe,
But I see it even if my husband does not:

Clemente will not say so,
He pretends he does not know what I mean,

But these nights in his sleep he has restless legs
As if only part of him is asleep

And the rest has got important work to do
And must get somewhere in a hurry.

He moves his legs in his dreams
The way a dog will sometimes bark in its sleep.

I stay awake. I watch him.
I try to help him, to hold and shush those legs for him.

He will not talk about it but he lets me try, now.
I pray and put on every medicine we can find,

Mud, too, and the bandages
Full of feathers and the smells made to cure things.

This restlessness disturbs his sleep all night sometimes.
He can find no end, no relief

Beyond tears, which do not work. In his sleep
He hits his legs to stop them, but this doesn't work either.

Watching him in the dark is a difficult thing.
That dog in him barks but at shadows and winds,

At anything that seems like something but isn't.
Because I think of his legs, because I see them,

Because I love him and we are two people
In one bed, when he thrashes his legs

It's as if he is hitting me or I am hitting him
When this happens. It's as if I feel what he must be feeling.

I'm all mixed up with his legs.
Whenever they hurt, my stomach hurts.

That's how we are, *comadre.* We're mixed up together.
But even with all this sorrow—

And how easy it would be to leave, you are right—
That's how life has made itself for the two of us.

This should not be our story,
Not after so many already hard years.

We should not be working even in our sleep—
Before now, I have always gone there for better things.

It's strange to you, perhaps, but I know
How I feel. I don't try untangling myself

To get away. It's the two of us, I think,
Together in the face of that thing.

That's how I feel. I have two hearts inside,
And some of his lungs—when I see something

That opens my eyes wide, and makes me breathe faster,
I hear him at the same moment

Take a deep, very fast breath with me.
It's always been that way.

I know what you mean, that I can leave if I want.
That's what it always looks like to the world.

But, *comadre,* if I tried to leave now,
It would be with his legs.

Explaining a Husband

They say two people aren't always two people.
That's what I've heard. Sometimes, two people,
They're the same person in two places.
And it's not that they have to love each other—
They don't. But no matter how they feel,
Whether they love each other or hate each other,

They still have to be together.
If not, they spend their whole lives, every day,
Looking around at everybody they pass,
On the chance that one person might look back
And hope that in the flicker of that moment
They'll both know it's them.

We're like that, I think, he and I, that husband of mine.
We're like that now, even if we didn't start that way.
We used to love each other.
But now it's something else, something more.
We know each other's life. And when we talk,
We are each other's story.

Good Manners

He had a sickness with a fever.
She tried to gather herself around him

To hold him, to gather herself
Enough to fit into what was missing in him—

What disease had taken,
Or what the mind had forgotten—

To replace what was taken so that no crime would seem evident,
Play some trick

To fool and to stop this fever,
Making it think itself inadequate,

Making it leave
Head bowed and with a little desperation.

She put herself, her body, around him
As she had always done in the small way

When he entered her,
That little and theatrical act,

But now she was big
And he was small.

She held him until her skin and her cells
Pushed into his.

She tried to let him put his fever into her
To take it away, to drain him, to calm him

Like so many times, only this was his life
Leaving him now, trying to stand in the heat,

To go out the door hand in hand as a friend with the fever,
To make no rude noises, nothing impolite.

To be good. But she was not his mother
Telling him to be quiet. This was his life

She tried to hold, and to hold again,
The steam of him rising like kite strings.

The Donkey Men of Sonora in the 1930s

In those days the *burreros* brought wood—
That's what we called the donkey men,

The *burreros*—and they loaded up their animals
Carrying bread, knife-sharpeners, razors, *pulque,*

That drink, in clay pots with loose-fitting cups as covers—
Not tight, or the *pulque* would explode the jar.

It was an acquired first sip
But popular enough in the quiet hillside canyons.

The donkey men did a little bit of everything
And heard a little bit of everything,

And as they replaced the sewing needles
They told the next person what news they knew

Passed on from the last person,
Sometimes on purpose, sometimes not.

Nobody loved them but everybody needed them,
And brought them in for coffee.

People bought things from them
Whether the things were needed or not, just to have them talk.

Amid everything, in the middle of all their news,
They were, as well, the keepers of love's fever

If not the practitioners.
With a boy's name here or mention of a girl's dress,

They simply kept the edges of the blade
Sharp and in repair.

Burreros—it was a funny word, like the men themselves.
After so many years together

The men were like their animals—
They, too, grew long ears, never looked up,

And they did the work nobody else could do.
They brought and did the small things, the corner things,

The things everyone put off or never got around to.
One of the *burreros,* Don Séptimo—

It was a name God gave me
Because no mother would, he used to say—

Don Séptimo used to tell me about a certain Doña María,
Who lived very far over there—he would nod to the south—

And I used to listen. He said she used to listen, just like me,
And wanted to know the same things.

I used to ask him questions.
He said that she asked him questions, too.

He used to tell me everything about her,
Especially her dreams of love,

But always pretended these parts of the conversation
Amounted to a casual observation,

Nothing pressing, even if it was what I was waiting for
And he knew it very well.

After all these years I have begun to see
She sounded a lot like me. I suspect

There was no Doña María. I always suspected it. Or else
There were a hundred of us. I don't know.

I just wanted to think there was somebody, to think
There was someone else like me in these hills.

Don Séptimo, even after all these years, like him or not,
Still comes around, though his donkey died a long time ago.

I always let him in. He still fixes the things
I need fixed—he knows the house so well—

And when he is done we sit at the kitchen table
For the rest of the afternoon, especially in winter.

Winter in the desert hills is quiet and smells of creosote.
Somewhere buried in the conversation we still talk of love.

Doña María, it seems, lives
In hope, even as an old woman and no matter what.

He tells me about her as we drink the coffee
Mixed with sugar,

Two of the things he has brought
And that make the afternoon bearable.

FOUR

Her Secret Love, Whispered Late in Her Years

Gravity wants me.
Gravity can't get enough of me.

Every time I try to leave,
It finds a way to make me come back.

It shows up wherever I go.
It's always been this way.

It keeps trying to wrestle me to the ground,
Sometimes catching me by surprise at the ankle.

It makes me laugh and sometimes I give in.
This thing that wants me,

This magnet to my body,
This amorous creature—it is a beast.

But I would miss it if it were not there.
I pretend otherwise, but it has turned me.

I am the one, now, being drawn to its arms,
Not simply it to me. I have heard it

Speak my name at last.
I have opened the front door to it.

When I was young, headstrong and full of stars
I ran from it, not ready for any embrace

More than the necklace those stars made for me.
But gravity, not the stars, caught my tears.

It has brought my hair down
And made my summer dresses fall from me.

Each time I was with child,
It whispered my name in the night.

As I grew a little heavier through the years
It only asked for me all the more.

I never told how I have felt it with me
In every step I've taken. Longest companion, unswerving,

It has never left my side, though all else has gone.
Gravity wants me, I used to think,

But I'm the one. I am the suitor I thought it was.
I say very nice things to it now. I am desperate

These days, desperate and ready
To lie down with it.

Daily Dog

The dog walks out the door on to the grass and the ground.
He walks as he's walked every day of his life, that walk.

This is his ground. This is his ground awake and asleep.
He walks and he wags, nothing sudden, nothing too much.

He does not fly through the air or slither on the stucco walls.
He does not jump from the ground into the limbs of the jacaranda.

He does not even lift his eyes to measure the possibility.
All-the-things-he-does-not-do—these weigh on him,

His small and straight spaniel body, nose down, nose down.
All-the-things-he-does-not-do he is starting to carry as extra weight,

This not-doing turning into more of itself,
Until he is no ballerina.

He does more of what he can do to compensate—
He eats more, he sleeps more, he looks into more bushes.

At a sudden moment he lifts his snout to the air
As if his nose were an ear that has heard something.

This is the fulcrum moment, every time.
In that siren-call minute is everything.

The lifted head, after so much hunching, so much
Attention to the ground: His lifted head threatens to unbalance him.

He lifts his nose to the wind, and it is not a sail
But the idea of one, and the idea-sail carries him a little.

The smell lifts him a little as well, this cartoon dog.
The wind and the smell and the curiosity

Aimed through him for the moment upward, they lift him
Slightly into this other place—a surprise to him,

This discovery of the continent of *up,*
A blue land in which he has lived no life but in dream.

This field empty of other dogs, this hovering, vast secret:
No plants, trees, no gravel, no hardness. It's good and bad.

This skyland, infinitely open, this biggest hole—
He looks at it with the two dark eyes of his nostrils.

He squints and lets these other eyes do their work.
He looks upward for a while, quietly. Intent.

With his eyes closed and his nose open,
He is stopped.

Every day he makes his decision.
Every day he is called to make it again.

The Dreams That Cried

Things become other things, she said.
It's what's inside them, I guess.
When I was little I always heard about the *onza* in the mountains—
It was supposed to be a combination of a mountain lion and a jaguar,
Something like that, something scary.
Now there's the *chupacabra,* which is everywhere,
Sucking the blood out of goats, and maybe people.
Those were the big stories.

But there were little ones, too.
I think they were worse.
The stories about the *niños de la tierra,*
I remember them most because they were matter-of-fact,
Those little pink spider or beetle animals
People would find when they were digging holes.
Everybody used to say that if you hurt one
It would cry like a baby.

I think people thought this because they looked like babies—
You would never hold one but when you looked at them
They had that face, or what looked like a little face.
Maybe they weren't really animals, after all.
Maybe they were dreams,
Dreams but inside the ground instead of the mind.
Maybe, right there,
We could hear something from our other world.

People Here Since Before Time

Some parts of the desert grow straight up,
Thin, the saguaros, the finger lines of cholla,

Ocotillo, the desert grasses, everything rising
As if a bad man with a gun had said *stick-'em-up!*

The things of the desert, even the hills themselves,
They grow this way for a reason

Kept secret by those who have themselves grown
With similar difficulty, people half-burnt and thin.

In the desert, they are not plants,
All of these sharp knives—

They are fingers of hard steam
Rising slowly from the floor of the desert,

Which tries but cannot keep it all inside.
The heat that rises is in no hurry.

Hurry here is a stranger, a tourist, an animal
Dead before noon.

At the end of the day, like it or not,
The sun noses itself to a stop here, and lingers.

This is the great secret of this desert:
The sun after everything comes here to rest.

A person might not believe this at first,
Because there is nothing to see.

But there is more to this place,
More at every turn. It's like in the movies:

The front is where the bar is, where the regular people go,
But in back, that's where the poker game is

And the sun wants in.
The proof is simple:

If you dig here, it's not water.
Dig, and the plumes of dirt from the spade are hot.

Farther down—it's true—there's humidity,
But it's not water, only sweat, only ever sweat,

A water not for drinking but meaner,
A water that is always leaving.

I was born of people from before
Who kept all this secret,

This search by the sun for a dark place,
This home to it, this place it could find

At least a bed, one big enough in all this space,
To lie down in. The coyotes and the scorpions,

The snakes, the tarantulas: They kept everything away,
Barking a warning even at the moon.

But the guest in the back room did whatever it wanted,
Then got its meager sleep. Nobody argued or told.

When it stumbled out of bed in the morning, after all,
It could be counted on to do more than its share.

The Chair She Sits In

I've heard this thing where, when someone dies,
People close up all the holes around the house—

The keyholes, the chimney, the windows,
Even the mouths of the animals, the dogs and the pigs.

It's so the soul won't be confused, or tempted.
It's so when the soul comes out of the body it's been in

But that doesn't work anymore,
It won't simply go into another one

And try to make itself at home,
Pretending as if nothing happened.

There's no mystery—it's too much work to move on.
It isn't anybody's fault. A soul is like any of us.

It gets used to things, especially after a long life.
The way I sit in my living-room chair,

The indentation I have put in it now
After so many years—that's how I understand.

It's my chair,
And I know how to sit in it.

My Ears Get Bigger from Listening

I can hear them all in the front room.
I can hear them talking.

They're trying to be quiet—it's for me, I'm sure—
But that always makes things louder.

The world is curious that way.
Sometimes it's inside out,

Like a pillowcase in the laundry.
Inside out—like how loud people are when they whisper—

That's when you see all the stitching and the edges,
The things nobody wants to show you,

All the roughness, everything you might want to hide
To make something seem better than it might be.

The trouble is, that's how a pillowcase is made.
That's how it stays together, even if you hide the seams.

Maybe whispering is like that—at first
It seems to hide a little of what we don't want to hear,

But the truth is very loud. It's a little rough, a little
Ragged, but maybe that's the way things are really made.

That's why when people tell you to be honest with them,
It feels like sleeping on inside-out pillowcases.

If they're whispering something out there, something
They don't want me to hear, it's probably for a good reason.

But when they do it—I can't help it—
My ear gets bigger, and I hear too much.

It's not a talent,
And it's never brought me very much joy.

But still, they're whispering, and even after all these years
I can't help but listen harder.

Later, When She Was Like She Was

She used to skip between all the things in her life toward the end,
Moving her lips as if she were an accountant balancing sums,

Though the words were more clear to her than to us.
Everything she said, she said two and three times, in an effort to be sure.

When she was like that, she was very good, very concentrated,
Busy so that no one dared to disturb her.

She had a strong face again in those moments,
The face she used to have.

If you needed her, you could put your hand on her shoulder,
And she would stir out of her state.

But she wouldn't stop talking,
Bringing something of the dream suddenly into the room.

She would say something continuing wherever she was in her story,
Whether or not you had been a party to its beginning,

Whether or not you would be staying for its conclusion.
It took a while, sometimes, to tell her that dinner was ready.

Having Forgotten about Eating

We had all kinds of citrus when I was young.
Apples, though, apples and pears were a luxury in the desert.
Bananas weren't being brought up from the south yet,
Except maybe a few of the very little kind,
The kind—you've seen them—only a tiny bit
Bigger than Brazil nuts. There were dates.
They were yellow on the trees, though, if you just left them.
They had to be tied up and covered with jute sacks
If you wanted them to ripen. Otherwise,
They would stay yellow for too long.
Then the birds feasted, and sometimes got drunk on them
Late in the season when they were soft inside.
There were some kinds of nuts.
And mountain onions, which we dug ourselves as children.
We ate rabbit, too, rabbits and hares, and chicken on Sundays.
Sometimes we had lamb—it was cheaper than beef then.
Eating, and thinking about eating, it takes me back so far.
We ate dove, too, and pigeons and quail and *pichiguila*—
These were some kind of duck, maybe rock duck.
Pichiguila. Whatever it was,
Just saying it always made me laugh.

A Song of the Old Days

The song on the radio was such a simple one,
A song from the old days.
Nobody else remembered it but her.

It belonged to the two of them,
But not because of what it said—
It belonged to them because of how it felt.

The song on the radio was such a simple one
Even then, even when the two of them
Hummed it into the skin of their mouths.

It belonged to the two of them
Because it lived inside the skin of their lips,
That song that even now spoke him to her.

A song from the old days
Meant something still, meant that once more
For a moment she was singing.

Nobody else remembered it but her,
Remembered the song or what it meant,
So that when she sang, it made no sense—

Even she could feel it. When she sang
It made no sense, not to the world nor to her.
It made no sense to say that he was gone.

FIVE

Clemente's Wife

Clemente. He is an old man
Like any old man.

His skin is black like a wool coat
With a little depth and some wear.

That wool coat has a stain,
I know you've seen it. I know

Where it came from. They say
One day some of Clemente's tears

Fell into the bacon grease
As he cooked himself a breakfast

Four wheels big with a running motor.
The tears exploded in that heat

Like small charges
In a small war

In that pan, the bacon itself
Responding: From somewhere

In that courtyard of artilleries
An exploding shell shot upward, reaching

The black wool coat
That was his heavy skin.

The coat was thick and the attack
Did not hurt him. The star

It rose and fell just under his eye,
Which itself might have been blinded.

But instead this brand made its mark—
A light-colored shape, a bag or a tear

The way tears themselves are a luggage
For water, for something leaving the body.

The stamp has stayed with him through the years.
He was crying,

And this mark makes him remember.
He wears his memory on the outside

This way, a note pinned to his coat
So that he should not forget.

Chance Meeting of Two Men

Mr. Clemente Ríos and Mr. Lamberto Díaz in a combined music
Raised to as loud as they could make their voices be
Announced to the world
Their love for each other.
Then after hugging they kissed each other on the cheek
And meant it. There was no mistake
Though it was neither scandalous nor revelatory.
They made their announcement after a crisp morning,
A long afternoon, and a spinning evening made of beer, blue
Wine, *membrillo*-flavored tequila, and cognac,
But a day made just as much
From the chili and smoke of conversation,
The butter of a pause and the chewing of agreement.
The curious thing is that they talked
About nothing in particular, and nothing
They said was news: The feel on a good morning
An old rope in the hand gives, sturdy pants that fit,
The smell of creosote after rain in the hills so strong
Even the rabbits come out to feel it in the air.
For Mr. Ríos and Mr. Díaz it was an uncommon day,
And they never spoke of it again.
But for an afternoon and an evening,
They were in each other's company
And in love with the world.

The Conversation of Old Husbands

She's gone, Clemente, I know. But I see her
In your eyes, I see what you're looking at
When you look away.
Where your eyes used to be
I see her.
Where you once had a tongue
You now wear a bow tie.
Old man, I understand.
I remember when you told me you saw her neck
And when you did it was as if she were outlined,
And not a part of the world,
Like a photograph lying on a newspaper,
Just there at that moment, bigger than the moment.
I thought of the dotted lines
They used to put around paper dolls
But they weren't dashes around her,
They were sparks. Still,
It was as if she were cut out from the world
Anyway, something saved off the page.
It's something you told me and that I've remembered,
Exactly as you said it.
Wherever she is
When you look at her, Clemente,
I see her too.

The Old Man Clemente Prays, Talking to His Wife Even Still

We have not exhausted all avenues, you and I.
Ventura, I have been thinking.

The people-who-count-people see only one of us,
Only me. But it's not true. We have to show them.

So I'm looking for you.
I used to want to come home to dinner with you

Just once again, but it's not enough now.
I want more. I will get the permission.

They make you fill out papers for everything here.
I know better. They would laugh at me

If I asked for the form that would bring you back.
They would laugh, and not even look.

You've heard them, but I know where to go.
I have an idea. I've been reading:

At any given time there are 100,000
People in the air

In airplanes above us.
That's where I would go first—

Who is the mayor of the city of air?
People like that, in their secret cities

They're everywhere. They will understand us,
They will know us. Listen to me,

We are wrong in that we listen for the secret citizens
Only with our ears.

Who is on the town council of that place
Inside us?

The earth and the sky,
We fill them with our dead,

From now and from the centuries:
In the city-states of the dead

Who is the vice-president?
I would write her. Is it you?

You would have told me.
People will be born, things made,

Roses and corn and green melons grown.
In the city of the future

Who is, and how could there not be,
A district coordinator of everything to come?

They are out there. We know it:
The governor of dreams

Has legislated against us,
More than once.

Ventura, I have been thinking.
I want to run for election to something

Inside, or something far away.
I want to be the high sheriff

Of the space between us. There is
Such a place. We both know it. And there are more:

It's somebody in the humming telephone lines.
It's somebody inside all those white envelopes.

When I think this
The needle on the compass turns like a propeller.

Everywhere is north.
The needle turns

In my hand, I hold on, it pulls me up—
Can you see me?—off the ground, toward the horizon.

No Instructions for Men like Him

There were no instructions for men like Don Clemente anymore.
No good directions existed on how to put them back together.

All the new things that had once built him were now worn.
Already some of his parts were missing,

An arm left at the ranch, a knee lost on a picnic several years ago.
Some parts got added that did not belong

But that were the only ones available to do a job.
Though he had a fine, dark blue suit, for example,

This last winter he could find no decent vest.
He wore a reasonable section of tablecloth in its place.

It did not match precisely, but did the job—and gave him ideas.
In fact, after all, it did the job of the vest and of a napkin both,

So that it was perhaps even better than what had been.
And given the tortoise quality of Don Clemente's skin,

So many folds and bends,
One of his elbows had been replaced by a nearsighted toad.

One could make it out bulging a little
Under his sleeve after he removed his coat.

The proof was easy enough:
If Don Clemente bent his arm there, it made a noise.

It may not in fact have been an actual toad under his coat sleeve—
It might have been something worse. Some said,

The protrusion was, rather, from too many years at the Molino Rojo,
His dedicated hours of putting that elbow to rest up on the bar,

That it was not a real toad at all,
That it was simply a callus and nothing more.

But there was other evidence, and very clear.
Others who had known him for many years said that, in point of fact,

A weak-eyed toad had simply followed Don Clemente home one day,
And he had not noticed. Yet to the world, its sound was unmistakable.

Given the fussing noise of this toad, the *basso profundo* they heard
But that did not come from his mouth,

Nobody could say, in fact, that there was not even perhaps
An assemblage of who knew how many other animals

Under his suit, some congregation of the small wild,
A herd of beasts alive and still at their work.

Everyone, after all, had heard the other noises he made
Every time he walked or sat down.

They knew the growls and small barks
When he moved at his leisure on the couch.

After a night of pleasant conversation—especially
Those nights when the conversation was about rain,

People still invariably looked at one another
Whenever he rose.

From somewhere in this man they could hear a whinny,
Every time, as if from a very small horse,

Something not more than an inch or two in height
Judging from the high pitch of the washboard sound.

All these things added together:
This was not simply an elbow or a vest

They were talking about, this was a man
Held together by things they could not see, only hear.

This was Don Clemente, who then, once risen,
Walked out into the night safe enough on all of his legs.

The Green That Calls a Person to It

So many bees, they would say, to keep themselves out of the gardens,
Bees and wasps, the sounds of moths, the general sway of the leaves.

All this makes a music after all, they said. That is what they heard
In the vines and flowers. Music, they agreed. Who, after all, was not

That romantic? Who could not agree that the air made its own song
Over there? But to go in, who would dare it? To go in:

This was to lose oneself to who knew what. The music in the gardens
Made itself, after all, out of everything, and would not behave.

To enter the gardens was to stay, and to return was to return
Unhappy at having left.

There was nothing left to do but whistle, to pick up the small
Melody of the green, to try and carry a little of its song for a while

Into the morning. Even this little bit was joy enough that he felt
Today. Joy was what he wanted, joy to lift itself from the gardens,

Joy to present itself to him, joy to enter and march his legs
In directions a little to the left or to the right of his everyday walk.

He wanted something of the gardens to transfer into him. He wanted
The gardens to become him in some way on these days as he passed them

Late in his life. But even to sing the sounds of the gardens
Was to give oneself over to them and what they held.

Still, every now and then, though he tried not to, he caught
A dim-light sound of hum. The echo found his ears

Even as he squinted his eyes in the late afternoon,
Even as his eyes saw nothing and were no good to him in this light,

The echo—sometimes harmonies or half-strains he thought
He could recognize—the sounds, they scared him, and afterward at night

He always put a pillow to his head as he slept.
Even so, he could not stop himself from following along

What the gardens had begun.
The songs invariably took him happily to childhood or to love—

And that was the difficulty.
Because in those things, he knew, sadness too had its song, a harmony,

A stalk very strong that held up high every flower
From the depth of the beds of the gardens.

Sadness too with joy had its song and the gardens with their love,
They made room for it all.

What Abides

The morning walk of an evening man,
It's different,

The movement is forward
But through a different air

And to a different place.
It's the walk that muscles remember.

In this way and with their own memory
The legs move without a body,

The legs walk outside
The legs, just for a moment,

Like the sharper memory
A nose has

Of a smell that once was,
Suddenly remembered.

But this moment this time this day
It is the legs

On a walk remembered back from sinew,
A walk brought back into the legs,

Walking even when the body has stopped,
Taking a path through the man,

Going where eyes have tried to be—
Where they tried to see, and did,

Then could not let go. There.
The fifth season, the meat heart

Pushed toward the inmost
Day, toward the red,

What blood and leaves are:
The season there, it is the afternoon

Of living most.
The night there is not darkness:

It is instead the place
Filled with the other things we think

Every time we think something.
It is a nice moment's twin,

A moment in the same moment
Rude wild unapologetic and strong.

The morning walk of an evening man,
That walk in the morning he takes

Every day is toward this night,
Beyond night and into memory

That hiding place
From which at any moment a man

Might jump,
Or from which a woman he once knew might smile.

On the morning walk of an evening man
He does not walk alone.

In that walk he is two men
And three, and four.

In that walk he is all the men
He has been

And all the men he has known,
All the women who have walked with him.

In that walk all of their eyes
Look in every direction,

Forward and back, at the ground and sky,
And into the quiet of the moment,

Into memory. It is in that quiet
The most dangerous animals lie.

The White

I saw a man at a flour mill once. Very nice,
He was also completely white, this man,
All white left and right and up and down—
It was from the flour dust we could see floating
Slightly in the sunlight but everywhere in the air.
As a result, the man in the flour mill was stained
White in all things,

Even, it seemed to me, under his white clothes.
He had a pale aspect on every side,
Even from behind—he had no shadow I could see,
The light itself in that room having stuck to him,
Building him of an inside-out mud made from dream,
Making him an inside-out man himself—

He was a photographic negative of a man,
The sort of thing as children we used to laugh at.
He was a ghost, exactly what we imagined,
The kind we all used to scream at and run from
As they stepped out of the dark riverside reeds
Or always seemed about to, with all that cricket noise.
Everything was turned around in him—

Hard work meant white under his fingernails,
Not black.
He left a trail of fair marks on the floor,
Not dirty.

His shoes were scuffed with chalky blemishes.
When he sweated he got creases—
They looked like skeleton fingers all over him.

That's me, now, all the things I saw in him,
The skeleton fingers. I feel as he must have
When I laughed at him those years ago.
I haven't thought about him since. But it's me,
Turned around altogether in things myself.
I hear my old laugh as I look in the mirror,
As I look at myself and see him.

SIX

The Theater of Night

It is 6:00 in the evening, a new-century evening
In the still-strong light of the desert.
The clock says 6, but I would not know it
From 5:30 or 6:30, not 7 or 5.
The numbers confuse what is not confusing.

The dark and the stars are coming, but not yet.
This is the time in-between, the gray time
The earth goes toward sleep but slowly,
Slowly and regardless of what we do,
In spite of the noisy people laughing next door.

Shadows begin to leave their jobs, tired
From a day without rest or recognition.
Poor shadows. They lie down from fatigue.
Cars begin to open their eyes. In these moments,
Stores begin to make themselves bright.

We make light what the world does not.
We walk into the night as if nothing has changed.
We have made the dark, in this way,
Not a blanket but a curtain, a temporary cover.
We pull it aside, peek in, and walk right through.

But we have been fooled. The lights go down
After all. We have walked into the theater of night,
By accident, we think. We make our way down the aisle,
We sit in the seat of dreams, and we watch.
We do not understand a thing.

It must be a foreign film, we conclude,
Even though there are no subtitles,

Even though it's us, our faces on the screen,
Very big, and funnier because of it—
We can see every pore and eyelash.

But what did you say? I couldn't make it out.
And what did I say? It makes no sense.
They look like us, but who are these people?
And what is this place? We want the lights
To come on. We want an usher to speak to.

Great-Grandmothers, Neatly Starched

Never young, she had been 94
Every day of her life for 94 years.
The invisible air she breathed was her own and no one else's.
The air she breathed lived in her clothing
And in her creases and underarms.
If from consternation she brought her arms quickly to her body,
They worked as a bellows: When that air came up from her,
It suddenly made people think of orange peels.

At the dinner table, she ate
Not so much to eat but to see that others did,
Getting up from the table for most of the meal.
Had she been a spider and left a thread
Everywhere she had been during a meal,
A thread trailing her around the table,
Over the table
To lift the pitcher of lemonade and pass the butter,

Under the table to retrieve the slipped napkin and fallen fork—
She very quickly would have spun a cocoon around us,
Silk in its momentary tenderness,
Silk in its miles-long fierceness, but silk—
Ancient, soft and strong,
Enough to have held all manner of and just enough food
High in the subhuman trees and soft
In the first and tender gardens

For all the years, all the centuries and hungers before now,
For all the animals of her kind. This was her life. She lived
Every day of it into her sleep. When she dreamed of herself,
She had eight legs, eight legs or eight arms. That's what
She felt. That's what she told me when she smiled at me

That tired half-smile of her half-open eyes.
She could not fall and would not.
And everything was all right because of it.

Her small face came to us in the night, flying by itself,
Her black clothing blending in with the black of the night
In the light darkness of our bedroom, so that her head
Seemed to float. She scared us.
Her hands were always coming at us, to fix this button,
To comb our hair, hard to straighten out
A wrinkle from our pants. She collected the wrinkles
From our clothing and wore them on herself.

She scared us and we began to imagine stories about her,
Stories different from what she told us.
She told us she had hands, of course,
But all we saw were Brazil nuts
Where her fingers should have been.
Her thick glasses made her eyes five times as big—
All the better to see you with, my dear—we thought.
She was the one who read us that story. We believed it all.

When finally she was gone she was not gone, nothing in her
In a hurry to leave. There she was still in the photographs,
And there, reflected in the shine of the onyx fruit basket,
Her color of brown in the dried-up leaves, which missed her.
There she was a hundred times
As we looked at the backs of the women in church,
All of them wearing her clothing.
There she was, the smell of oranges everywhere.

The Cures of Green and Night

Evening. The medicinal smells
Rise in the steam of the chamomile tea,

The steam's white arms
Reaching to me as I remember being reached for

By the arms of a nurse when I was five,
Asleep in the hospital.

Those weeks and always after when I was sick
My grandmother made me the tea, very hot.

And from that tea her own white steam arms rose,
From inside the tea itself, some hand,

An arm and some fingers, reaching out.
This hand of hers was an open hand

But also an entertainment, the hand in the steam
Wobbling like a puppet's.

It made me laugh. I let the hand touch me,
Tickle me as it reached and held me,

Its long fingers circling around my head,
Holding me a moment to an invisible shoulder,

This hand and this arm from the tea, this hand
The hand that had made the tea,

That had struck the match
And had wiped itself on my grandmother's apron.

It was her, her hand, I knew it even like this,
My grandmother's third hand.

Drink, she would say, and nothing more.
Chamomile, my grandmother's medicine

For children, and we were all children
In the luxuries and excesses of her kitchen

Whose smells and tastes were as much garden,
Her bread made from leaves and blossoms

After rain. I have walked and I walk even now
Through this garden so filled with its mulch

I am above the ground walking on it.
At night, asleep, when sleep has come,

I have walked the hard walk
On the easy ground of this old wood.

The cure is like that, in that place
Green with the eyes open, green with the eyes closed.

Its green is chamomile with mint leaf,
Its particular fragrance a smell different

Like trees remarkable for the sounds of a bird
You cannot see, its sound

A song coming from the inside of the leaves.
The cure has always been that

And nothing more. It is still
These counsels of the small world:

Break open a leaf and a song comes out,
A song in the leaf in the hand.

Coffee in the Afternoon

It was afternoon tea, with tea foods spread out
Like in the books, except that it was coffee.

She made a tin pot of cowboy coffee, from memory,
That's what we used to call it, she said, *cowboy coffee.*

The grounds she pinched up in her hands, not a spoon,
And the fire on the stove she made from a match.

I sat with her and talked, but the talk was like the tea food,
A little of this and something from the other plate as well,

Always with a napkin and a thank-you. We sat and visited
And I watched her smoke cigarettes

Until the afternoon light was funny in the room,
And then we said our good-byes. The visit was liniment,

The way the tea was coffee, a confusion plain and nice,
A balm for the nerves of two people living in the world,

A balm in the tenor of its language, which spoke through our hands
In the small lifting of our cups and our cakes to our lips.

It was simplicity, and held only what it needed.
It was a gentle visit, and I did not see her again.

Clemente and Ventura Show Themselves, if Just for a Moment, in Their Son

Margarito was a serious man
But for one afternoon
Late in his life
With serious friends.
They adjourned to a bar
Away from the office
And its endless matters.
Something before dinner,
Something for the appetite
One of them had said,
And the three of them walked
In long sleeves
Into the Molino Rojo.
The cafe's twenty tables
Were pushed together
Almost entirely
Or pulled apart barely,
Giving not the tables
But the space between them
A dark and ragged shine
Amid the white tablecloths.
The tables
And the spaces they made
Looked like pieces of a child's puzzle
Almost done,
A continent breaking, something
From the beginning of time.
To get by them
Don Margarito had to walk
Sideways, and then sideways

Again, with arms outstretched
And up.
It was a good trick of the place
Conspiring with the music
To make the science
In this man's movement
Look like dance.

Two and a Half Men

Don Margarito walked with a cane.
In this way he was more of a man.

He had more parts.
My grandfather, he was more of a man

Or less of a horse, somewhere in between:
Without the tail, but with

The neck.
And who knew what else.

If his half-horse eyes had in them
The blue fire of a race

In the green field of air,
At the same time he could not be appeased

With sugar. In his face, that look said
He put salt in his coffee.

Two shakes: One for the sugar,
One in place of the cream.

Don Margarito in the Twenties about to leave
On a campaign for the Revolution,

Singing the *Internationale* one morning
And after drinking his coffee,

To wipe his mouth
He reached for a handkerchief

Into the vest pocket of a dream
He had put on like a coat

To go out walking his walk to the woman.
And it was that woman. The other.

He got mixed up.
It happens just like that—

One reaches for a handkerchief
And comes back with a French bread.

Here is the story. Out there
Somewhere, there was this other woman:

She was not my grandmother.
The next day

The calendar in him got turned,
As if the wind had got into him.

As if he had opened his mouth
And the wind came in—like in the movies—

Turning all the pages of the calendar
In a few seconds. Suddenly

It's another year and another day.
He acts like Saturday

On Monday now.
Hello he says to me

When I pass him
Dead since the Fifties,

Hello, when I pass him, there
Standing, like anyone else on the street.

The Drive-In of the Small Animals

1

The pink light of a desert late afternoon, middle July,
The gold light, the peach light, this curious, this peculiar,

This sepia-in-color still-life light lasts for two minutes,
Three minutes, too late for you—if you were not there,

Lucky enough to be in this world and see it for yourself.
Photographs cannot find these shades in the catalogue of what they know.

They offer a rendering of something else instead. Something normal.
Standing in this light we are transfixed at this small glimpse of the other

World, our world, but for this one moment seen from the outside in.
The monsoon-season rain is almost here, and evening, too, everything

A half inch farther than late afternoon.
The rare-light gets us ready for the infrequent rain

We hope will come, and today it does.
After the several minutes of moisture, the desert world

Lets everything out, as if the heat had been a locked cage
And water was its skeleton key.

2

The geckos on the back porch
Hide, waiting for dark and dinner,

Waiting to see the curious other light we turn on
In place of the sun, a light that brings the bugs out to look.

We are their circus.
They stand at our windows and look in.

They cling to the screen doors like boys
Playing a game of hanging on the chicken wire

Trying to get a better look at the batter.
The bugs, their eyes are big from what they see.

Sometimes they need more than two eyes
To take in what we are, what we do, what will come next.

Some small creatures have invented saw-teeth for their arms
To hang on more easily, more comfortably,

Well set for the longer time of a whole evening
So much is their astonishment,

Their shaking of their heads and rapt attention
In not wanting to miss a minute of us.

3

So many creatures have done what we cannot,
So many tiny angels, so many stick-legged scientists.

Some have grown sharp wings from their backs.
They try to get in and get out before we see them,

To get some memento, or just to get closer for a moment
To see if we are real. We look so big,

Magnified by the glass of the windows.
Some small beasts have developed suction cups

Glued in some mysterious fashion onto their hands and feet.
They climb the sides of buildings like fancy house-burglars.

They climb high enough with those cups,
Then stop and shift gears, finding a second use for them,

A use as plain as day: They use the cups to listen,
Placing them like a glass against a wall—

They've seen us do it before and they've paid attention:
They've seen us watch the 1940s third-rate movie detective

Holed up in a cheap motel do the exact same thing.
They know how this plot works.

He listens through the glass, hoping to get the lowdown
And the skinny and the goods on the galoot and the tomato

Up to no good in the room next door.
It always works.

4

When what we say is funny, is good, or brings tears
To all their eyes, when we say something that will start

The evening's story moving, the beasts listen harder
Using everything, their hands and feet both.

They see harder, using that kaleidoscope trick of their eyes.
They want to catch every word, every nuance.

Sometimes the streaming, starstruck crowds of teenaged roaches
Make their move, hoping for a crumb souvenir

We left at the top of the sink at the end of the second act.
They try to be quick, not get in the way,

Not ruin the play of us by some hick mistake,
No talking too loud or sneezing over everyone,

No calling our names out loud when we come onstage.
No. They try to be a little smarter than that

Even with all the pushing, all the egging-on:
Go ahead, one would say, *I dare you to spit on somebody.*

5

It's true that many want to come in—
It's in their nature and they cannot help it.

Some try to get bit parts in the show:
They apply as walk-ons or come early

To be in the live audience.
They try to be as animated as possible,

Wiggling and fluttering what they have,
Crawling quickly, coiling and uncoiling.

Some want to be extended into the next season.
The mice and ants have tried.

Cats and dogs have had some modest success.
Some pigs and monkeys, some lizards and snakes, some fish—

Very quietly.
Other beasts are content to stay outside, to keep a distance:

All that noise we hear out there
In the strident woodwind of the crickets,

That conversation of theirs, their incessant bragging—
Claims about who was there for what episode,

Declarations about the real reason the gun is in the drawer—
That gossipy magazine of animal words,

The unsettling imitation of electricity's sound
Made by the Saturday night horror-movie-aficionado cicadas

Dressed as their favorite characters,
Dressed and ready for a good time

In big-goggle eyemasks and see-through lab coats,
The thousand ballads of the million wannabe bit-part actor birds.

6

But the stories of the audience are there to be told as well.
Sometimes a bird hits a window straight on,

Just to see if it will work,
If this blunt, brute act will turn the tide,

Making someone inside take notice of the outside
And give a bird its showbiz chance.

A bullfrog under the back porch light after a hard rain—
That Trojan horse of the small world. Big amphibians,

They try their best. But nobody lets a frog into the house.
These frogs, the big mistake of their moist appearance:

They will spend another several centuries
Evolving into something else, something

More appealing, something that will be let in.
Patient things,

They are thinking of starting pretty soon,
Now that they feel reasonably certain

This disguise as a beating heart with legs
Doesn't work.

7

Some beasts hang off daredevil ropes spun from the ceiling.
Some hover on hardworking helicopter blades.

Some eat their way through the walls to get a good spot,
A personal box seat with wood snacks and paint liquor.

All of the curious beasts, they are outside and forming lines.
This house—it's this house but it could be anybody's house—

This house is the drive-in of the small animals.
After all is said and done, the hordes of them,

They don't want to come in so much as to watch,
To see what will happen next—

In pink light, in monsoon humidity, even in rain
They cannot go away.

They are hooked on the soap opera
We have given them

Through the centuries,
Interested even with so many incessant reruns.

They are like anyone.
They can't wait to see how the story ends.

About the Author

Alberto Ríos, born in Nogales, Arizona, is the author of nine books and chapbooks of poetry— including *The Smallest Muscle in the Human Body,* a finalist for the National Book Award— three collections of short stories, and a memoir, *Capirotada,* about growing up on the border. Ríos is the recipient of numerous awards, and his work is included in several hundred national and international literary anthologies, along with many public art installations. His work is regularly taught and translated and has been adapted to dance and both classical and popular music. Ríos is presently Regents' Professor and Katharine C. Turner Chair in English at Arizona State University, where he has taught for twenty-four years. Currently living in Chandler, Arizona, he has lived all over the state and was recently designated an Arizona Historymaker by the Arizona Historical League, a lifetime achievement award.

Copper Canyon Press wishes to acknowledge the support of Lannan Foundation in funding the publication and distribution of exceptional literary works.

LANNAN LITERARY SELECTIONS 2005

June Jordan, *Directed by Desire*
W.S. Merwin, *Migration*
W.S. Merwin, *Present Company*
Pablo Neruda, *The Separate Rose*
Pablo Neruda, *Still Another Day*
Alberto Ríos, *The Theater of Night*

LANNAN LITERARY SELECTIONS 2000–2004

John Balaban, *Spring Essence: The Poetry of Hồ Xuân Hương*

Marvin Bell, *Rampant*

Hayden Carruth, *Doctor Jazz*

Cyrus Cassells, *More Than Peace and Cypresses*

Norman Dubie, *The Mercy Seat: Collected & New Poems, 1967–2001*

Sascha Feinstein, *Misterioso*

James Galvin, *X: Poems*

Jim Harrison, *The Shape of the Journey: New and Collected Poems*

Maxine Kumin, *Always Beginning: Essays on a Life in Poetry*

Ben Lerner, *The Lichtenberg Figures*

Antonio Machado, *Border of a Dream: Selected Poems*, translated by Willis Barnstone

W.S. Merwin, *The First Four Books of Poems*

Cesare Pavese, *Disaffections: Complete Poems 1930–1950*, translated by Geoffrey Brock

Antonio Porchia, *Voices*, translated by W.S. Merwin

Kenneth Rexroth, *The Complete Poems of Kenneth Rexroth*, edited by Sam Hamill and Bradford Morrow

Alberto Ríos, *The Smallest Muscle in the Human Body*

Theodore Roethke, *On Poetry & Craft*

Ann Stanford, *Holding Our Own: The Selected Poems of Ann Stanford*, edited by Maxine Scates and David Trinidad

Ruth Stone, *In the Next Galaxy*

Joseph Stroud, *Country of Light*

Rabindranath Tagore, *The Lover of God*, translated by Tony K. Stewart and Chase Twichell

Reversible Monuments: Contemporary Mexican Poetry, edited by Mónica de la Torre and Michael Wiegers

César Vallejo, *The Black Heralds*, translated by Rebecca Seiferle

Eleanor Rand Wilner, *The Girl with Bees in Her Hair*

C.D. Wright, *Steal Away: Selected and New Poems*

For more on the Lannan Literary Selections,
visit: www.coppercanyonpress.org

The Chinese character for poetry is made up of two parts: "word" and "temple." It also serves as pressmark for Copper Canyon Press.

Founded in 1972, Copper Canyon Press remains dedicated to publishing poetry exclusively, from Nobel laureates to new and emerging authors. The Press thrives with the generous patronage of readers, writers, book-sellers, librarians, teachers, students, and funders—everyone who shares the conviction that poetry invigorates the language and sharpens our appreciation of the world.

Major funding has been provided by:
The Paul G. Allen Family Foundation
Lannan Foundation
National Endowment for the Arts
Washington State Arts Commission

For information and catalogs:

COPPER CANYON PRESS
Post Office Box 271
Port Townsend, Washington 98368
360-385-4925
www.coppercanyonpress.org